PHILOSOPHICAL CONTEMPLATION

Theory and techniques for the contemplator

Loyev Books

PHILOSOPHICAL CONTEMPLATION

Theory and techniques for the contemplator

by

RAN LAHAV

Loyev Books

ISBN-13: 978-1-947515-94-9
ISBN-10: 1-947515-94-2

Copyright © 2018 Ran Lahav. All Rights Reserved
Cover photograph © 2018 Ran Lahav

Loyev Books
philopractice.org/web/loyev-books
1165 Hopkins Hill Road, Hardwick, Vermont 05843
USA

Contents

Preface	vii
Chapter 1: Why philosophical contemplation?	1
Chapter 2: What is philosophical contemplation?	7
Chapter 3: Depth, inner depth, and the Lu experience	17
Chapter 4: Practical principles	27
Chapter 5: Preparing for contemplation	38
Chapter 6: Procedures of text-contemplation	46
Chapter 7: Typical contemplative experiences	58
Chapter 8: After contemplating	64
Chapter 9: The philosophical contemplator	68
Chapter 10: Texts for contemplation	74

Loyev Books

PREFACE

My first encounter with the practice of text-contemplation was more than two decades ago, at a Trappist contemplative monastery. I visited the monastery for a few days of peaceful retreat, and I was immediately captivated by the monks' quiet and solemn attitude, even though I never believed in their religious faith. In the following years, the monks kindly allowed me to stay in their monastery for longer periods of time and share their quiet daily life, without ever trying to convert me to their religion. I am grateful for their open hearts and for giving me this life-changing experience. For many years I would spend weeks or months at a time in the monastery, and the quiet life of contemplation would touch me deeply and inspire me. I learned what it means to live a contemplative life and to nurture inner silence.

Among other things, I also learned how to read a text in a contemplative way, opening within me a space of inner listening and letting the text speak in me and awaken in me deep insights. At first I used the monks' books, but after a while I started feeling uncomfortable with these religious texts. If I did not believe in the doctrines which they proclaimed, how could I full-heartedly immerse myself in them?

I started experimenting with other kinds of texts, and I soon discovered those that worked better for me. I realized that for a text to work, it had to speak about fundamental reality – but without dogmatism. This realization led me to experiment with passages from philosophy books, and I quickly found them to be what I was looking for. Philosophy, after all, explores the basic dimensions of existence, and it does so non-dogmatically. At that time I was a junior philosophy professor at university, so I was already accustomed to reading philosophy.

The discovery that philosophical texts could serve as material for contemplation was a turning point for me. Since then, for more than twenty-five years, I have been contemplating almost daily on a selected text, often from Western thought, although sometimes also from Asian or Western-religious traditions. I found this to be a profound source of inspiration, insights, and plenitude. Throughout the years I have also taught and mentored groups and individuals in this practice.

The present booklet is based on my personal journey in the realm of philosophical and spiritual text-contemplation. It offers some basic concepts and guidelines for those who feel the yearning to embark on a similar journey. In a certain sense, contemplation has no guidelines, since it is much more than a technique – it is born in one's inner depth, it is animated by the yearning heart, and it has its own unique rhythm and life. Nevertheless, guidelines may be helpful if one takes them as a starting point, not as strict rules that must be followed to the letter.

Chapter 1

WHY PHILOSOPHICAL CONTEMPLATION?

We practice philosophical contemplation because we yearn to connect with a source of wisdom and understanding that is greater and deeper than our usual thinking patterns. Philosophy is about the fundamental dimensions of reality, and philosophical contemplation can help us transcend our ordinary boundaries.

Philosophy cannot provide us with solutions to life-issues, or final theories about life, or guidelines for happiness or success. Its power lies not in its capacity to provide answers, but to make the process of searching fuller and richer. Through philosophical contemplation we reach out towards greater horizons.

But in order for this to happen, we must assume an inner attitude that is open and attentive, and that is not limited to detached theoretical thinking. It is easy to philosophize in the abstract without letting philosophy touch us and inspire us. That is why in contemplation we philosophize not primarily in our abstract thoughts (although this, too, is valuable), but from our inner depth. In other words, we do not just *discuss* philosophical ideas, we *contemplate* them, which means that we open ourselves to their power to act within us and to awaken dormant dimensions of understanding.

When contemplation is successful, the result is a powerful experience: the experience of being touched by a greater reality, the exhilaration of taking part in the broader horizons of life, and thus a sense of immense realness. Philosophical contemplation is part of a love story. It emerges from a yearning which, as Plato explains, seeks the highest reality. We practice philosophical contemplation because, to use his terminology, we are animated by Eros – by the longing to connect with truth and realness. We contemplate because we are in love.

One might say that this is a "spiritual" urge and a "spiritual" quest. I have no objection to this word, as long as we remember that this quest has no gurus or religious authorities or holy scriptures, no doctrines or saints or angels, no divine revelations or miracles. It is a quest that is always open and free of dogmas, always still on the way towards the furthest reaches of human understanding.

The use of philosophical texts

If we want to contemplate on fundamental issues, we cannot start from nothing, as if nothing before us has been said on the topic. We should remember the philosophical voices of the past. The writings of deep philosophers throughout history are humanity's attempt to address basic life-issues, which is what philosophy is about. They, like us, are part of humanity, and our philosophizing is part of humanity's never-ending encounter with basic issues of life.

A deep philosophical idea – of Plato or Spinoza, Schopenhauer, Bergson – is not just somebody's private opinion. A thinker is not an independent atom, but part of human reality. His or her thoughts come partly from a personal search, partly from the culture's attitude to life, and in a large part from human existence in general. In this sense, thinkers write not just from themselves but from humanity.

For this reason, in philosophical contemplation we contemplate on the writings of philosophers of the past (and present). When we contemplate them, we are taking part in the greater human choir. This does not mean that we must agree with these philosophical voices or decide which one is "correct" and which one is "incorrect." It means, rather, that we "resonate" with them like one singer with other fellow singers.

Thus, as philosophical contemplators we relate to historical philosophical texts differently from ordinary university philosophers. For many academics, historical ideas are abstract theories, historical constructs, finished philosophical products. In contrast, for us contemplators, the voices of past philosophers do not belong only to the past. They are part of a discourse which is still going on, part of an ongoing encounter of humanity with reality. The voices of the past continue to resonate in the present, and if we want to take part in philosophy, we must join them and resonate with them.

When I contemplate on philosophical ideas or texts – not when I repeat them like an obedient university student, not when I analyze them like a historian, not when I agree with them or disagree with them, but when I resonate with them personally and creatively from the depth of my being – then I am facing reality. This is the reality which all deep philosophers conversed with (and human beings in general, although usually with less awareness and depth). When I resonate from the depth of my being with the philosophical voices of great philosophers, then philosophy becomes a genuine encounter with the great ocean in which I am a little wave.

Self-transformation

Philosophical contemplation is transformative because it helps us change our state of mind. It develops a fuller awareness of hidden dimensions in us and in our encounter with reality. Our familiar self is only the surface of our being, only a limited part of our potentials. We are more than we seem to be. Philosophical self-transformation helps us realize those potentials.

The realization that everyday life tends to be superficial and limited, and that philosophy can help transform it towards fullness and depth, has been familiar throughout the history of philosophy. Many important philosophers have written about the power of philosophy to help us on the road to self-transformation. According to Plato, for example, philosophy can show us the way out the "cave" in which we are imprisoned towards the highest level of reality. Stoic philosophers like Marcus Aurelius developed contemplative-philosophical exercises to overcome psychological attachments, to connect with the true self (or "daemon"), and to be in harmony with the Logos of the cosmos. Spinoza contends that philosophy can lead us to an understanding of reality that is a state of blessedness which he calls "an intellectual love of God." Rousseau's philosophy of education explores ways to protect us from alienating social forces and help us cultivate our natural self. Nietzsche's philosophy encourages his readers to overcome their small self – the petty, frightened, herd-animal which we are – and live a noble and passionate life, which he calls the overman. Emerson's philosophy calls us to open ourselves to the over-soul, a metaphysical source of creativity and inspiration that operates within us. Bergson's poetic philosophy teaches us to see the poetic and holistic qualities of life; and the list goes on.

Despite the differences among those philosophers, they evidently had a similar vision: Philosophy can show us the way to transform our state of mind and awaken deeper dimensions of our being. This age-old vision is at the heart of philosophical contemplation. When we engage in philosophical contemplation, we realize that philosophical ideas have a tremendous power to change us. For the philosophical contemplator philosophical ideas are precious sources of growth and self-transformation.

Chapter 2

WHAT IS PHILOSOPHICAL CONTEMPLATION?

Philosophical contemplation is a practice of reflecting on fundamental life-issues from our inner depth. We think not from our opinions and ideologies, not from our automatic thoughts, but from an aspect of our being that is deeper within us than our normal thinking patterns. This inner depth, when awakened, is a fountain of insights, inspiration and plenitude, but it is usually dormant in everyday life. Contemplation serves to awaken it, focus it, and cultivate it.

Philosophical contemplation has a long history in the West. It was practiced by philosophers in the ancient Greek and Roman world, particularly by Stoic philosophers who developed a variety of spiritual exercises to cultivate the true self within themselves.[1] In later historical periods, contemplation was taken over by religion, as can be seen in Christian, Jewish and Moslem writings of the Middle Ages. It thus became mainly a religious activity, colored by religious images and doctrines. For example, it was often practiced with religious

---

1. Pierre Hadot, *The Inner Citadel*, Harvard University Press, Cambridge 1998.

scriptures, and was often interpreted as communication with angels, saints, or even God. Although it is likely that some individual philosophers continued practicing some forms of non-religious contemplation, contemplation stopped being part of mainstream philosophy.

The practice of philosophical contemplation has been revived in recent years in the field of philosophical practice, a field which aims at making philosophy relevant to the lives of ordinary people. This old-new practice is done primarily as a group activity – "the philosophical companionship" as I dubbed it while developing this format.[2] But philosophical contemplation does not have to be practiced in a group. It can also be practiced by a solitary individual, perhaps even more powerfully and deeply. In fact, my own daily contemplation of the past two and a half decades has been mainly a solitary practice.

What is contemplation?

In casual speech, the word "contemplation" is often used to refer to any kind of thinking, but strictly speaking it means a special kind of intellectual-spiritual activity. It is intellectual in the sense that it

---

2. Ran Lahav, *Handbook of Philosophical Companionships*, Loyev Books, Hardwick 2016.

is about ideas, and it is spiritual in the sense that it involves deeper aspects of our being that are outside our normal psychology. Contemplation therefore requires us to assume a special state of mind, usually with the help of exercises that activate deep parts of ourselves. Combining these two elements, the intellectual and the spiritual, we may say that in philosophical contemplation we work with philosophical ideas from the depth of our being.

To better see this, let us note that not all kinds of thinking are the same. In everyday life we sometimes think by actively focusing on an idea and grasping it clearly, while at other times our thinking consists of many ideas floating in our mind blurry and vague, barely noticeable. Sometimes thoughts come to our awareness spontaneously as if by their own power, while at other times we control them or produce them with an effort of the will. Some thoughts are quick and excited and noisy, while others are quiet and slow. Some thoughts are linear, while others rush quickly in a million directions, even if we try putting them in order. Some thoughts are separate from our emotions, while others are excited and angry or jealous or joyous. Evidently, different kinds of thinking have different powers to act in us, to motivate us, to influence our state of mind, and to move us to action. Two thoughts may have the same content – they may be expressed by exactly the same words – and yet they may do very different things in us.

For our purpose, especially important are those thoughts that are deep within us and that touch us deeply. "Deep" is of course a metaphor, and we will later explore what it means. Roughly speaking, however, "deep" thoughts come from sources that are more basic or primordial than our ordinary psychological patterns. These thoughts are not yet structured or "tamed" by our thinking mechanisms, and as a result we experience them as touching the whole of us, as precious and inspiring, and as being especially real. Yet, in everyday life they are quite rare. Even when they do appear, we are usually too busy to pay much attention to them. Our minds are full of plans, worries, phone calls, e-mails and social media, and all these tend to drown our deep thoughts and suffocate them.

Deep thoughts require an inner space of silence and listening, which is the opposite of the avalanche of thoughts and images that fill our minds in ordinary moments. Contemplation is a practice that helps us maintain this inner space, and thus to nurture those special thoughts that arise deep within us. When we practice contemplation, we are attentive to our inner depth and to the insights that rise from it into our awareness. But contemplation is not a passive listening. It is, rather, an active dialogue between me and my inner depth. In this inner dialogue I may recite certain phrases to "invite" new insights, I may reflect on relevant concepts or distinctions to sharpen these insights, I may try to articulate those insights in words, I may divert the flow of thoughts to a certain direction, and I may ask myself questions.

Such an inner dialogue is not necessarily philosophical. But if we focus the process on philosophical ideas or texts, then it becomes philosophical contemplation.

What is philosophical in contemplation?

What do we mean when we say that philosophical contemplation is "philosophical"?

Philosophy is a long historical tradition involving numerous thinkers who have developed throughout the ages a wide range of ideas and theories. In the West, it was born more than twenty-five centuries ago and since then has been continuously developing and changing. Although this rich tradition cannot be squeezed into a simple definition, nevertheless we can characterize it in an approximate way by looking at its history. Philosophy is whatever so-called "philosophers" have been doing throughout history. If we limit ourselves, for the sake of simplicity, to Western philosophy, then several general characteristics of philosophy become apparent:

First, all philosophers investigated fundamental issues about life and the world. Their discussions were not focused on personal facts about John or about Mary, or on local issues about this city or that village, but on general issues that deal with the foundation of our understanding of life and reality: What does it mean to know? What is the relationship between the mind and the body? What is true love? What is the good life? What makes a moral act moral? And so on. This is the first characteristic of philosophy.

However, philosophers are not the only ones who address such issues. Poets and novelists do so as well. There are many works of literature that deal with the meaning of life, with the nature of love or friendship, or with moral issues. Therefore, additional qualifications must be added to distinguish philosophy from literature and poetry. One important difference is that unlike poets and novelists, philosophers respond to life-issues in a systematic way, trying to compose a universal, clearly stated, organized account of the topic at hand. One might say that philosophy involves constructing *theories*, but this characterization is a little too narrow. Several important philosophers, such as Socrates, Kierkegaard, and Wittgenstein developed networks of ideas that may be too loose to count as theories. Certainly, all theories consist of networks of ideas, but some networks of ideas are too unsystematic to count as theories. We should better say, therefore, that the second characteristic of philosophy is that it seeks to address fundamental issues by constructing a coherent network of ideas about them.

But these two characteristics are still not enough. Philosophy is not the only field that offers systematic networks of ideas about fundamental issues. Religion and theology, too, do it. Religion and theology, however, base their ideas on faith and authority – on faith in holy books, for example, or on the authority of a church. In contrast, philosophy investigates freely, without commitment to any presupposed belief. To be sure, philosophers are human beings and as such they are not free from biases and unwarranted presuppositions, but at least they try to be free from them as much as humanly possible. In this respect, philosophy is similar to science, which likewise attempts to conduct free investigations that are free of unwarranted presuppositions. Science, however, bases its investigations on empirical observations, while the laboratory of the philosopher is the mind.

This is, then, the third characteristic of philosophy: It investigates freely, using primarily the power of the mind. The notion of "power of the mind" is a bit vague here, and intentionally so, since philosophers differ in their methodology. Some philosophers like Spinoza use logical thinking, others like Bergson use intuition, some like Reid and Moore use common sense, still others like Husserl use introspection, and other philosophers use reasoning in various other senses. Yet, they all seek to address fundamental issues by using the mind, without relying on faith on the one hand and empirical observations on the other.

Two additional complementary characteristics should be added here. The fourth characteristic is that in order to do philosophy (or to philosophize), it is not enough that you copy your ideas from another philosopher. Philosophizing is a creative activity. It is essentially an investigation, and as such it typically generates new ideas. Fifth, all major philosophers developed their investigation in dialogue with other philosophers, usually by reading previous writings and responding to them, correcting them, or opposing them. Philosophy is a tradition of intellectual discourse, and every thinker who belonged to this tradition participated in this discourse. You cannot be part of this tradition if you don't know anything about it and do not relate to some of its members.

It may be possible to add additional characteristics, but for our purpose the above five are sufficiently close to what philosophers have been doing for over the past 2500 years of Western philosophy. To conclude, then, philosophy is a discourse that addresses fundamental issues of life and reality by composing coherent networks of ideas (or theories), using the powers of the mind in a creative and dialogical way. This should also apply to any contemplation that aspires to be philosophical. A contemplation can count as philosophical only if it follows this five-fold characterization.

One might object that I am treating the notion of "philosophy" too strictly. Philosophy has no clear boundaries or definition, and there is nothing wrong with extending it beyond its traditional realm. My answer to this objection is that there is indeed nothing wrong with practices that deviate from the philosophical tradition, but in that case they would not be philosophical anymore. No doubt, there may be wonderful practices that do not share all five characteristics, such as psychotherapy and yoga, which are beneficial to many – philosophy is not the only good thing in the world – but these practices do not belong to the Western tradition that is called philosophy. Philosophy is not just an arbitrary name – it refers to a specific tradition that contains a certain body of writings and certain methods and practices. If you want to belong to this tradition and enjoy its treasures, then you must practice the kind of things of which it consists.

Philosophical contemplation is philosophical because it is faithful to the nature of traditional philosophy, although of course it does so in its own unique way. It deals with fundamental life-issues through dialogue with other philosophers, usually by contemplating on their philosophical texts. It is creative and based on powers of the mind, because in the process participants develop new creative ideas as they arise from their inner depth, and as they are later organized and articulated in discussion. In this way they compose networks of ideas that relate to basic life-issues.

Chapter 3

DEPTH, INNER DEPTH, AND THE LU EXPERIENCE

Earlier I said that in philosophical contemplation we think from our inner depth. What, then, does inner depth mean?

Depth as an invisible source

The expression "deep thoughts" can already be found in the Bible. Psalm 92, verse 5 reads: "*O Lord, how great are your works, and your thoughts are very deep.*" Notice that "deep" is applied here to the noun "thoughts," and that expressions such as "a deep thought" or "thinking deeply" are used today too. In contemporary language we also talk about a deep idea or insight, a deep book, and deep conversation. Interestingly, we don't usually say "a deep painting" or "a deep dance" or "a deep dinner." This suggests that depth is connected to wisdom and understanding. A deep idea has depth – it contains more than its face value, because it has an additional dimension of meanings beyond the apparent surface. It is the tip of an iceberg of a vaster domain of wisdom.

Emotions, too, can be deep. We sometimes speak about deep love, a deep hurt or pain, deep hate or anger. If you feel deeply, then you feel "from the bottom of your heart" – from a source or dimension within you that includes much more than a specific feeling, from a source that includes much of yourself. A deep emotion involves a rich ocean of inner life, and it expresses it and gives voice to it. Thus, for an emotion or thought to be deep is to have "depth" – to be the expression of some hidden vastness.

"Deep" (or "profound") is of course a metaphor. When we speak of a deep thought, we don't mean that it is located "under" a surface in a geographical sense. Nevertheless, this metaphor is not arbitrary. It is based on an analogy with the depth that lies under the surface of the earth or of water. The things that are happening in the depth of a pond, for example, are largely hidden, and they are visible only vaguely or indirectly. We may notice that something is going on in the depth of a pond – a moving shadow, a flicker of light – without being able to tell what exactly we are seeing.

Likewise, in the depth under the surface of the earth there are invisible roots and bulbs, worms and ants, mice, and who knows what else – an entire underground world in fact. The roots that are hidden in this underground are the sources of trees and plants, the hidden origin of visible things. Indeed, we sometimes talk metaphorically about "the root of the matter" or "the root of the problem." Roots are something we do not see directly, but they give birth to the visible forests and meadows. The underworld is a hidden, vast and complex reality that is different from the visible things that are here with us, and yet it gives birth to them, and they are expressions of its hidden powers.

Interestingly, very few philosophers have attempted to analyze the notion of depth, even though the words "deep" and "depth" appear quite often in philosophical texts. The French philosopher Gabriel Marcel is one of the few who did discuss this notion.[3] He suggested that speaking about "depth" is a metaphorical way of speaking about one's original source – one's "home country" so to speak, which is far away and yet is here in one's blood. This analysis is in line with the interpretation of depth offered here.

Inner depth

A person, too, may have depth. We talk about a deep person or a superficial person. We also talk about our "inner depth" – the depth that lies "inside" us. A person's depth is the hidden dimension in a person which makes him a deep person. It is a hidden realm of rich and complex wisdom or meanings that cannot be easily captured, defined, exhausted, and yet it

---

3. Gabriel Marcel, *The Mystery of Being*, Henry Regnery Company, Chicago 1960, Volume I, Chapter 9.

manifests itself in the person's visible behavior and words.

The existence of inner depth is not merely a speculative theory. We can experience it in ourselves, or, less directly, as a quality of another person. Thus, we sometimes feel meaningful insights and emotions appearing "deep inside us" and "rising" to our awareness. This suggests that we sense that there is a hidden realm within us, and that we feel it as a source of special meanings and thoughts that can inspire us and move us, fill us with insights and wonder, and make us more than our routine psychological self.

Our inner depth is largely hidden even from our own view. Although as conscious human beings we are aware of many of our thoughts and emotions, we do not experience our depth directly. We may feel ourselves inspired by an invisible source, we may feel the result as a powerful understanding that invades our awareness, we may even know what triggered this upsurge (perhaps a sentence we have just read), but the inner source itself remains largely hidden from us. Yet, we normally experience it as something precious and inspiring. In moments of creativity we may even feel that "something" is giving us words to write, images, ideas, musical sentences. This is exactly the semantic source of the word "inspiration" – something breathes its life into me.

This hidden realm which we call "inner depth" cannot be identified with our usual self, which consists of our familiar patterns of thought and emotions, our normal opinions and desires, our everyday tendencies and sensitivities or insensitivities. That is why we feel, when our inner depth is awakened, as if something different from us is acting within us and through us. For a limited time – for a few seconds or minutes or even hours – the normal sources of our feelings and thoughts are no longer fully in charge. New resources in our being take over.

The Lu experience

Philosophical contemplation is intended to help awaken our inner depth. The contemplator pushes aside the automatic thoughts and images that typically swarm the mind and silently attends inwardly, usually while reflecting on a short philosophical text. The result is that new fundamental insights often rise into consciousness like bubbles of air rising from the depth of a lake to the surface of the water. They are often experienced as especially significant and enlightening, even if their content is not very new. They may be accompanied by a powerful sense of inner silence, of marvel and awe and even sacredness, of intense presence and realness, or what in general can be called a sense of *preciousness*.

Earlier I said that contemplative insights come from a source that is deep "within" us, but this may be disputed. One might point out that in contemplation we often experience our insights as coming from a source that is outside ourselves, from a greater source of intelligence. A number of participants in contemplative groups told me that they had felt as if something bigger than themselves had touched them, stirred up their inner depth, and sometimes inspired them with surprising words or ideas.

I call this *the Lu experience*. I use the word "Lu" to refer to the source that is presumably beyond myself and that sometimes acts in my inner depth. The word "Lu" is intentionally without meaning. I chose it to indicate that it refers to a source that is beyond all words, beyond the verbal mind, at the root of one's thoughts.

The Lu experience might be taken to imply that the source of our contemplative insights is external to us, lying not only outside our familiar psychological self but our inner depth as well. It is as if our inner depth receives its insights from an external source of intelligence; as if it is the "sense organ" through which we "perceive" ideas from the bigger reality which I called Lu.

This might be what our Lu experience tells us, but the question is how seriously we should take it. Experience is a subjective impression, but does it reflect the facts, or is it a mere fiction?

I would like to leave this question open and let the reader decide how to interpret the experience of "beyond myself," namely the Lu experience. Practically speaking, for the purpose of practicing philosophical contemplation, this interpretation does not matter very much. Whether our contemplative insights come from our inner depth or from outside us, they are still coming from sources that are beyond our usual psychology, beyond our normal self, and are worth pursuing.

A suggested interpretation of the Lu experience

Nevertheless, I would like to suggest my own personal way of interpreting the Lu experience. In general, I prefer to avoid interpretations that are too extreme to be reasonable.

On the one hand, it seems to me unreasonable to dismiss the Lu experience as a mere subjective fantasy. We must admit, I think, that contemplative understandings often consist of rich and insightful ideas that can be meaningfully shared and discussed with others. They cannot reasonably be rejected as a mere private fiction. The special intense quality of the experience suggests a source of understanding or intelligence that is different from our usual self.

But the other extreme is equally unreasonable. There seems no basis to speculate that the Lu experience comes from exotic sources such as angels or spirits or a universal mind that whispers its ideas in our hearts. Such interpretations seem to me too fanciful and unnecessary.

In order to avoid both extremes, I find it sufficient to say that contemplative insights originate from sources of meaning or wisdom that are broader than my ordinary psychological structures. Or, to put it metaphorically, that these understandings originate from horizons that are broader than myself. This assumes a realm of wisdom and meaning that extends beyond the boundaries of my normal self, and that resonates in my inner depth and inspires precious insights. Put differently, I am like a wave in the ocean, resonating with the movements of the great waters.

Note that the idea of a source of insights that lies beyond myself is not as strange as it might seem to be. Certainly, ideas are not just psychology, and they cannot be reduced to psychology. Mathematics, geometry, and logic are simple examples of ideas that are not mere products of subjective psychological processes – they were valid even before any intelligent being was around to think about them.

Although contemplative insights are not the same as mathematical formulas, they are similarly more than subjective psychological impressions.

Many important philosophers believed that our mind can grasp realities that lie beyond our psychology, whether through reason, intuition, or other forms of understanding. The Stoics, for example, believed that reason can reveal the Logos that ruled the cosmos. Kant contended that reason can reveal the basic categories of the phenomenal world, the world we find around us. Many additional examples can be given.

Thus, there is nothing especially strange in the idea that contemplative insights are anchored in a reality that extends beyond personal feelings and opinions, beyond the domain of psychology.

However you choose to interpret the Lu experience, we should note that it feels precious. The understandings which it raises in us are experienced as having a special realness, a deep meaning and a special importance. Many religious texts describe the experience in religious terms: "God spoke in me," "the Holy Spirit inspired me," "the saints taught me." This testifies to the special quality of the experience.

This preciousness of the Lu experience is one important reason why as contemplators we aspire to be attuned to our inner depth and yearn for it. This is the yearning Plato calls "Eros," which propels us to leaving our narrow cave and reaching out towards the highest reality which Plato calls the True and Good and Beautiful. This is the spiritual longing that motivated a Neo-Platonist like Plotinus to transcend the material world and unify with the One. This is also the yearning that motivates many religious people from all religious traditions to reach out towards their God. We, as free-spirited philosophers, do not commit ourselves to any of these doctrines – to Platonism, Neo-Platonism, Christianity, or any other religion. We acknowledge and cherish the yearning for the greater horizons of being, the longing of the little wave for the ocean, without speculating on what this ocean might be. We do not want to belittle our Lu experience by turning it into a mere dogma or conjecture.

Chapter 4

PRACTICAL PRINCIPLES

In philosophical contemplation we contemplate on texts that deal with fundamental issues of life and reality, in other words on philosophical texts. These texts orient us towards the broadest horizons of meaning and understanding.

Philosophical texts may not be the only ones that raise basic issues. Sometimes we are led to reflect on such an issue under the influence of a poem, a religious text, even a popular song. Yet, philosophical texts lead to a fuller reflection because they contain a rich, focused, systematic, and coherent network of ideas.

Philosophical ideas as generative seeds

In a contemplative session we typically use several paragraphs from a philosophical text. Not every text is appropriate for contemplation. A desirable text is concise, accessible, includes a complete idea, and is written in precise and rich sentences, possibly poetic ones. Such texts can be found in many philosophy books, even when the book as a whole is dry and verbose. Wonderful gems are hidden in many unexpected places. In my own contemplations I have used texts by Plato, Marcus Aurelius, Plotinus,

Kierkegaard, Nietzsche, Emerson, Bergson, Jaspers, Marcel, Buber, and many other thinkers.

However, what is required for philosophical contemplation is not so much a special text but a special inner attitude. This is an attitude of listening carefully to the text – to its concepts, to its words and their melody, to the progression of the sentences, to the images and the rhythm – without opinions, without judging, without agreeing or disagreeing. We savor the text as we savor a wine or food, or as we listen to poetry or to a piece of music. We do not treat it as a theory that is correct or incorrect, because we regard it as one voice in the rich choir of human ideas. We do not regard is as a statement that aspires to describe the way things are, because we are looking for depth, not for precise descriptions.

Such an attitude is very different from our usual relationship to ideas. In everyday life we express an idea when we want to state an opinion we believe to be correct. We love to possess and declare opinions about the political situation, about the environment, about life after death, about human rights and justice, and we declare them as true and defend them against opponents.

Similarly, in mainstream philosophy one regards philosophical ideas as statements or theories about the way reality is: as theories about the nature of true love, or about the meaning of words, about the good life, about the foundation of knowledge. One philosopher may believe in utilitarianism while another in duty ethics and a third in virtue ethics; one philosopher may support a foundationalist theory of knowledge while another may a coherentist theory. In this respect, philosophical ideas are regarded as similar to scientific theories, in the sense that they claim that our world is this way and not that way. A theory functions like a picture: It is meant to represent or mirror objective facts.

There is nothing wrong with this way of understanding scientific or philosophical theories, but it is not appropriate for philosophical contemplation. Once we regard a philosophical idea as a statement or theory, then there are not many ways to relate to it: Either you agree or disagree with it, either you think that it is an accurate description of the way things are or you think that it is not. A theory is the end-product of an investigation, a finished set of statements that excludes any different statement.

In contrast, in contemplation we want ideas to be dynamic, not finished conclusions. We want them to be the beginning of a movement of thought and not its final product; to be seeds of further thinking and not final fruits. We realize that ideas have a power to inspire us, to give birth to new insights, to resonate within us and develop and grow. This is why in contemplation we do not agree or disagree with philosophical ideas, and we do not declare them to be true or false. We carefully examine what they might mean to us and where they might take us, we open ourselves to them and listen to what they do within us, and how they change and develop in our minds.

Improvisational thinking

In order to keep ideas dynamic and ever-developing, we can relate to them through "improvisational thinking." In this kind of thinking we start with the text, but do not necessarily remain in the text. We are free to compose variations on the text just as a musician improvises around an original musical motif. The original text is the starting point and reference point for alternative lines of thought, not a final authority.

Imagine, for example, that we contemplate on Socrates' famous speech on the topic of love in the dialogue *The Symposium*. In this speech, Socrates describes how love develops from a "low" kind of love for a physical body to a higher love to beautiful souls, to an even higher love for Beauty itself. If we regard this speech as stating a theory, then we are stuck in a specific doctrine about love. We can agree or disagree with it, we can apply it to specific situations, and that is all.

Alternatively, we can regard Socrates' speech as a first musical phrase in an improvisational concert, so that our role as fellow musicians is to resonate with it. After Socrates has played, it is now our turn to add our own musical phrases by composing ideas that are variations on his original idea, ones that are not exactly his theory but are analogous to it in certain respects. For example, we may start with Socrates' idea of gradual progression from material love to spiritual love, but apply it to another concept such as happiness (from physical pleasure to spiritual joy) or self-awareness (from awareness to the body to awareness of the spirit). Or, we may start with Socrates' dichotomy of the specific versus the universal – but with respect to a different concept such as wisdom (wisdom about specific matters versus universal matters). Or, we may add to Socrates' picture an additional element that is not in his original speech, such as self-love. Thus, Socrates' original idea of the stages of love may inspire an analogous or complementary idea, similar in certain respects but different in others.

The resulting contemplative ideas would no longer be Socrates', but they would be inspired by him. Thus, in improvisational thinking our contemplative ideas are nurtured by an original text and they grow out of it creatively, preserving some of the complexity, richness and depth of the original.

The polyphony of philosophical ideas

Theories, as I said, are like "pictures" or "maps" of reality, in that they attempt to mirror the way things are. The central metaphor here is visual: A theory corresponds to reality just as a picture or a map mirrors a given landscape. But this visual metaphor is not suitable for philosophical contemplation. To contemplate on a philosophical text, we need to treat ideas as being more flexible and dynamic, and for this reason it is better abandon this visual metaphor, even if the writer of the text himself had it in mind. Instead, we can adopt an auditory or musical metaphor and think of philosophical ideas not as descriptions ("pictures") that correspond to reality, but rather as voices or sounds that come from reality.

The auditory metaphor has a very different inner logic from that of the visual metaphor. A picture resembles the original, but the sound of a song-bird does not resemble the bird. The sound of a river is not a map of the river and the voice of a singer does not mirror the singer. Although there is an intimate connection between the sound and its source, there is no resemblance between them. The same applies to contemplation: We do not regard philosophical ideas as "maps" or "pictures" of reality, or as "corresponding" to reality. For example, a philosophical idea about love may come *from* the experience of love, but it does not need to mirror it. It may relate to love in many complex ways.

Furthermore, the auditory metaphor of sounds or voices tells us that no single philosophical idea is the correct one. While a picture or a map – like a theory – may be the correct one, this is not the case with a sound. The same object may emit a variety of different sounds, and these do not contradict but rather complement each other. Think, for example, of the different sounds that may come from a tree – when a soft wind murmurs through its leaves, when a storm thrashes its leaves against each other, when rain drops tap on it, when its trunk creaks as it sways in the wind. The auditory metaphor suggests that ideas can compose a polyphony of different but compatible meanings, instead of competing maps that contradict each other.

Moreover, the auditory metaphor also suggests dynamic changes and development, as opposed to a map or picture which is a finished, stable product. Like the changing sounds of a tree in the changing weather, ideas, or networks of ideas, may change in meaning and develop as time goes by, as we ourselves change, and as our ways of encountering reality change.

Thus, when we treat philosophical ideas not as pictures mirroring reality but as voices of reality, we can relate to the many ways in which reality resonates in us. This enables us to see life as a rich polyphony of meanings that are dynamic and non-exclusive, complex and multi-faceted. We are no longer forced to choose between theories – between utilitarian ethics and duty ethic, between Descartes' mind-body dualism and Berkeley's idealism, between empiricism and rationalism. We can listen to them all and appreciate them as different voices in the complex polyphony of reality. This allows us to truly contemplate on philosophical ideas.

Contemplating on personal matters

Philosophical contemplation often focuses on a philosophical text, but not exclusively so. In the process of contemplating, we may go beyond purely philosophical ideas and relate to a personal experience that we had yesterday, or to a recent family incident, to a personal hope or distress, and so on. However, to the extent that our contemplation is philosophical, we never lose sight of the broader horizons of life. We always contemplate on a personal experience or issue in the context of the larger philosophical perspective on fundamental dimensions of reality.

In this respect, philosophical contemplation is very different from psychological counseling. In psychology, the subject-matter of the counseling is a particular personal situation: the client's anxiety, the client's trauma, disturbing behavioral patterns, and so on. In philosophical contemplation, in contrast, our main subject-matter is a fundamental life-issue, in other words the universal symphony of human existence. If we contemplate on a personal matter, it is always against the background of this general symphony.

For example, in the course of contemplation I may reflect on a recent argument I had with a friend, but as part of a philosophical contemplation on the concept of friendship. Or, I may contemplate on my sense of meaninglessness, but in relationship to a philosophical text about the meaning of life.

This does not mean that I try to *apply* a philosophical idea to my personal experience. In philosophical contemplation we do not impose philosophical ideas on life, and we do not ask whether a personal matter "fits" a philosophical idea. Applying philosophical ideas to concrete situations is done in so-called applied philosophy, which is very different from contemplation.

In philosophical contemplation we may let an idea resonate with our personal experiences, so that it sheds new light on them and gives them new meanings. And conversely, the experiences may enrich and modify the idea we are considering. Picturesquely speaking, we "place" in the contemplative space an idea and a personal experience side by side, and we then let the two interact with each other and generate new understandings and meanings. For this reason, when we wish to contemplate on a personal experience, it is not necessary to find a text that would match it precisely. Even when the selected experience and the selected idea seem foreign to each other, they would probably interact in rich ways and give birth to creative and surprising insights.

Maintaining a contemplative attitude

Philosophical contemplation is based on the power of philosophical ideas to move us, touch our inner depth, and awaken within us a dormant dimension that is open to new horizons of understanding. But of course, philosophical ideas do not always have this effect. When we chat casually, or make silly jokes, or are preoccupied with our smartphone, it is very unlikely that we would be touched and inspired, even if wonderful ideas are being uttered by people around us. In order to contemplate we should maintain an appropriate state of mind – an inner attitude of focus, inner silence, attentiveness.

To be sure, philosophical ideas may sometimes inspire us even without preparation. It happened to many of us that, even in the middle of a shallow chat, some sentences struck us deeply. But this is rare. Usually we need to "help" the philosophical idea to act within us by assuming a state of mind that would make us available to the idea's potential power.

This state of mind can be called the "contemplative attitude." Like everything that is deep, it cannot be produced with a fixed mechanical technique. Assuming a contemplative attitude is an art. It requires practice and experience, personal growth and maturity, and probably some talent as well. Whether you are a beginner or an experienced contemplator, awareness to your state of mind is very important.

Chapter 5

PREPARING FOR CONTEMPLATION

We cannot contemplate fully if our mind is busy with everyday thoughts. It is therefore helpful to start a contemplative session with a short centering exercise to disengage ourselves from our normal rhythm and attitude and to open an inner space that is separate from the tumult of everyday life. This exercise can also serve as a ritual for preparing the mind and body for the transition. A centering exercise does not have to be long or complicated. Sometimes it is enough to sit quietly for a few moments and feel the silence enveloping your mind. Sometimes, however, you might feel the need for a more elaborate and focused exercise.

Air Meditation

In this centering exercise, the column of air in my body serves as a metaphor for my entire self. I start by focusing my attention on my breathing in my head and nose, then I gently slide down to my mouth, throat, chest, stomach, thighs and even further below. While doing so, I experience myself descending from my normal superficial self downwards into my inner depth. The result is a sense of calm centeredness which stays for a while after the exercise.

To start this meditation, sit comfortably on the floor or on a chair, your back comfortably erect, and your hands and legs placed in a symmetric position. It is best to close your eyes to facilitate concentration. Breathing should be somewhat slower than normal but without a special effort.

After a few moments of silence, focus your attention on your head, which is where you usually feel yourself located. In your mind feel your forehead, ears, eyes, temples. Then gently move your attention to the beginning of the column of air – to the nostrils, and feel the air as it flows in and flows out. While doing so, don't *look* at the nostrils (in your mind's eyes) but rather *be* there.

After three or four slow breaths, gently move your attention to the front part of your mouth, and feel the air coming in and flowing out, brushing against your tongue and lips. Again, don't look at your mouth but simply feel yourself resting there. Try inhaling through the nose and exhaling through the mouth, and if this is not too difficult, continue breathing like this for the rest of the exercise. Your breath should be a little slower now, but not constrained.

After three or four more breaths, gently slide in your mind to the back of your mouth, rest there, and feel the air flowing in and out, brushing against the roof of the mouth and the root of the tongue.

Next, gently move your attention to the upper part of the throat. While being there and feeling the flow of air, you may also sense the muscles of your throat and possibly the tension and strain that might have accumulated there.

After three-four more breaths, sink to the bottom part of the throat, feel the flow of air and the muscles, and feel how your breath is becoming even slower. From there continue to your chest, where you will feel the vastness of its space as the lungs contract and expand, and from there to the stomach, where you will feel the muscle movements that activate the entire column of air resting on it. If you remember not to look (in your mind) at those body parts but rather be in them, you will now experience yourself situated much lower than your head and eyes, where you usually experience yourself.

Now gently continue to your buttocks and thighs and feel the touch of your pants on your skin and the pressure of your body against the chair. Although you are now under the column of air, you can still feel the muscles reverberating with the breathing above them.

Lastly, make the final descent: From the thighs gently sink down to a point below your body, underneath your chair, perhaps a meter (three feet) underneath you. Metaphorically, you are now below your usual self, at the root of your being, in the point of silence or wisdom. If the exercise is successful, you will feel yourself in profound inner silence.

Keep this point of silence in your mind when you start contemplating.

Body-parts meditation

In this centering exercise you direct your attention to your body, focusing on one organ at a time, while gently sliding from your feet upwards to the top of your head. To start the meditation, sit on a chair symmetrically, close your eyes, and focus your mind on your right foot. You may feel its pressure on the floor, the touch of the skin on the shoe, the throbbing of the blood, the muscles. After a few seconds gently move up your attention to the ankle and feel it in your mind. Then move to the knee, and then the thigh. Next move to the left foot, the left ankle, and the left knee and thigh. From there, continue shifting your attention to the pelvis, the stomach, the chest, the right shoulder, the arm, elbow, wrist, hand and fingers. Now move to the left shoulder and go down along the arm to the left fingers. Then go back to the chest and ascend to the throat, the chin, the nose, the eyes, and the top of your head.

Your mind should now be focused and free of thoughts and images. You can now pick up the text and start your contemplation.

Self-instructions

In this centering exercise you give yourself a sequence of instructions, each one directing you to assume a specific bodily and mental attitude.

A good starting point is the instruction "Notice." Say it to yourself in your mind, and obey it by noticing everything that is happening in your awareness: the continuous flow of thoughts and images, the background worries and plans in your mind, your bodily tension and bodily stance. Also notice what has been going on in your awareness during the past few hours, your hurried actions, the many words you uttered and heard, your efforts and worries. Notice this non-stop avalanche and make it all present in your awareness.

The second instruction is "Stop." Say it to yourself in your mind, and feel yourself obeying by stopping all your mental activity. You are no longer projecting yourself to the future – planning, expecting, waiting, preparing, starting. You are right here now, no longer running around for errands and chores and appointments. You feel yourself at rest. If the thoughts in your mind continue running, dissociate yourself from them: They are not you. Don't fight them – let them run wherever they want while you stay here in yourself, present, immobile.

Third, tell yourself "Let go." Relax your hands and arms, relax the tension in your entire body and your mind, feeling as if you are releasing whatever you have been holding.

Next, tell yourself "Trust," and in response feel your entire body safe and protected. You are no longer on guard, no longer ready to defend itself. You are now being cuddled in the arms of reality, so to speak, trusting it like a baby in its parents' arms.

Now tell yourself "Open myself," and feel yourself being opened to the entire world without the usual boundary between me and not-me.

Next tell yourself "Expand," and feel yourself flowing towards the world. You are no longer just here, because you are spread out over there, everywhere.

Lastly, instruct yourself: "Empty," and feel yourself pulling yourself back from the center of your world and leaving it empty. You have stepped back, so to speak, from your usual central position in your world and have opened an empty space within yourself. You are no longer the main actor in your own world. At the center of your self there is an open space of listening, like a clearing in a forest. Silently listen to anything that wishes to appear or speak in this clearing.

At this point you should feel silent and attentive. You can now start contemplating.

Needless to say, you may change this list of instructions and create your own.

Presencing

The above centering exercises involve considerable self-control and structure. Alternatively, you might prefer a more relaxed exercise. One possibility is to simply sit quietly for a few minutes. However, the absence of focus might allow your mind to lose itself to thoughts and images and start wandering to plans and concerns. A better alternative is therefore to sit quietly, let your eyes glide over objects in your room, and make them intensely present in your mind. This is called "presencing": Instead of seeing a chair or a pen as an ordinary thing in your spatial environment, you focus on it as if was a special gem. You intensify its visual appearance in your awareness and make it present.

Do this exercise gently, without excessive effort, letting your gaze glide spontaneously from one object to another, stopping occasionally on an object and presencing it, and then continuing to the next object.

After a while, your mind will no longer be busily involved in the world as usual.

Chapter 6

PROCEDURES OF CONTEMPLATION

After the centering exercise, the mind is probably focused, attentive and quiet. We are now ready for the contemplation itself.

In a certain sense, there are no techniques for contemplation. The contemplative act comes from our yearning to go beyond our limited self and connect to a deeper reality, whether within us or beyond us. This yearning is a form of love, and just like love it cannot be produced by instructions. It has its own life and rhythm within us. You cannot force yourself to love somebody through a technique.

Nevertheless, techniques or procedures may help focus the contemplative spirit and strengthen it. A marriage therapy cannot create love out of nothing, but it can work with existing emotions and longings to nurture and orient them.

Silent lesson

Silent lesson is perhaps the most important procedure of text contemplation. If successful, it produces insights that are experienced as deep and precious and as coming from our hidden depth into our awareness. This procedure is an adaptation of the *Lectio Divina*, a form of text contemplation that has been developed by Catholic monks in the Middle Ages, and which is still practiced today in Christian circles.[4]

In the silent lesson, we silently read a short philosophical text and listen inwardly to the understandings that rise in us in response. The text provides us with the philosophical materials to work with. It also serves as a central axis of contemplation that helps us maintain focus and centeredness. And it gives us a network of ideas which resonate and grow within us throughout the contemplative process, revealing new unexpected meanings and adapting themselves to our own life. As a result, we may experience the text speaking to us and "teaching" us new insights. Hence the name "silent lesson."

It is best to choose for this procedure a short philosophical text, about one or two pages long, that is condensed and even poetic. You don't need to agree with what the text says – the text is one among many "voices" of human reality and a starting point for developing your own insights.

There are several versions of the silent lesson, some for a single reader and some for a group. In the following version, the basic idea is to discern in the

---

4. For modern versions of *Lectio Divina* see Gustav Reininger (ed.), *Centering Prayer*, Continuum, New York 1998.

text a wide array of meanings, and then to consolidate them into a focused understanding by concentrating on one sentence or idea.

a. *Preliminary reading*: Go over the text to understand its literal meaning. Try to maintain a calm and gentle state of mind, so that all your actions and thoughts flow gently and attentively.

b. *Noting a manifold of ideas*: Go back to the beginning of the text and read it again silently, but this time very slowly and carefully. Listen to each word, as well as to the ideas and images that it evokes in your mind. Don't force onto the texts any interpretation or analysis – let the text speak in you. Don't worry if your mind remains blank and empty of ideas – insights have their own rhythm, and the main thing is the act of listening itself. Whenever you feel an idea surfacing in your awareness – a sentence, a word, an image – just note it. "Noting" an idea means acknowledging it, as if saying to it "Hi, I saw you!" After a few seconds or minutes, when you have finished noting, gently continue reading. After reading the text two-three times, you will probably have a collection of ideas that have emerged from the text. Sometimes this process is more fruitful if you jot down your understandings as they appear in your awareness.

c. *Contemplating a selected sentence*: As you were listening to the text, a certain sentence may have caught your attention. It may have seemed to you particularly meaningful, intriguing, moving. Focus on that sentence and reflect on it in relation to the array of meanings which you have noted before. Do not try to analyze this sentence or decipher its meaning – let it hover inside you and listen to it. Treat it as a candy that you savor in your mouth without trying to crack it with your teeth. To do so, you may recite the words several times, or learn them by heart. Another excellent way is to carefully write them in a calligraphic manner, while maintaining a focused inner silence.

d. *Consolidating*: Now that you have generated an array of meanings or ideas, it is time to switch direction: consolidate the many into one, the multiplicity into a unity. Your goal now is to find a unified, coherent understanding that is central to what you have noted – not a summary (how can you summarize ideas that are very different from each other?), but a meaningful center around which everything seems to revolve. Gently go over the words and ideas you have previously noted and "encourage" them to consolidate themselves into a unified insight. The emerging central idea may be about a general issue, or about a situation in your personal life. As before, do not impose your interpretations – be attentive and let the ideas do most of the work.

It often helps to ask yourself a question and then inwardly listen to an answer within you. Keep the question in your mind while gently going over the text several times, with a special attention to the sentence you have selected.

Don't be disheartened if no new understandings arise. The point of this contemplation is not to end up with a product – a new idea or a novel interpretation of the text – but the contemplative process. The inner attitude of peaceful openness to your inner depth is valuable in itself.

e. *Exit*: Slowly let your attention dissolve, and be careful not to terminate the session too abruptly. As you relax and stand up and return to your daily activity, try to maintain for a while the contemplative attitude and to keep in your mind some of the words and insights that have touched you. A good way to do so is to write down some of the ideas you are taking with you.

Vague reading

There are several alternatives to the procedure of silent lesson. One of them is vague reading, in which we read a short text while intentionally keeping our mind unfocused and vague. In this way, new understandings arise within us not through our normal analytic thinking, but through a side-channel of our mind. This procedure works well when you read a new text for the first time.

After centering yourself, sit quietly and start reading your selected text slowly, savoring the words as they flow through your mind. Your mind should be attentive but in a receptive way, without any effort to grasp, analyze, or figure out. If a sentence is not clear to you, don't stop and don't read it again. Act as if the text is not addressed to you – your task is only to narrate it, not to understand. It is as if you are reading the text for somebody else who is listening to you.

With this inner attitude, read steadily and note gently the images and ideas that might float on the periphery of your awareness. At the end of the reading, switch to a focused state of mind. Try consolidating the ideas you remember either by writing them down or articulating them in your mind. To attain an appropriate inner attitude, treat these understandings as precious "gifts" that have been given to you by your inner depth.

Recitation (*Ruminatio*)

This procedure is intended to enable ideas to rise to your awareness in response to a repetitive reading of a selected sentence over and over again.

After centering yourself, start reading a philosophical text of about a page in length. Read it slowly and carefully, pronouncing the words in your mind or whispering them. While reading, notice a sentence or brief passage that attracts your attention, that touches or intrigues you – in short, that "wants" to tell you something.

After you finish your first reading, go back to this special passage and read it again, slowly and attentively. Listen to the words themselves – to their sound, their rhythm, to the way they are pronounced in your mouth. This kind of reading is very different from normal reading; normally we "look through" the words to their meaning without paying attention to the words themselves.

Keep reading the same passage over and over again at least six or seven times. Don't be alarmed if you feel bored or annoyed – this is normal. Listen inwardly to ideas and images that surface in your awareness. Treat them as precious "gifts" given to you by your inner depth. At the end of the reading you may consolidate them and articulate them in words, either in your mind or in writing.

Resonating with ideas

This procedure is designed to connect ideas from the text with a personal experience from your life. The point is not to interpret your personal experience, not to impose on it philosophical ideas, but to let philosophical ideas "converse" with your personal experience. In this way, the text will reveal hidden meanings in your personal experience and enrich it.

In the first stage, read the selected text quietly and attentively. Identify a short passage that attracts your attention and read it several times. Notice some of the main concepts that compose this idea. For example, if you selected Jean-Paul Sartre's "The look" (a section in his book *Being and Nothingness* about how we encounter another person), you may notice the concepts of *the look* (the other is somebody who looks at me), the concepts of *subject* and *object*, the concept of *objectification* (the other person's look makes me an object), the concept of *freedom* (a subject is free, unlike an object), and so on.

In the second stage, recall an event or situation you experienced recently which seems to bear some connection to the text. It need not be completely similar – on the contrary, it is best to choose one that is somewhat different.

In the third stage, keep in your awareness both your personal experience and the text, and let them be present in your mind side by side. Reflect on them in detail, including the concepts which you derived from the text, as well as the small details of the experience. Listen inwardly to the way the two interact with each other, how they shed light on each other, how they differ or agree. Don't analyze, don't impose your ideas, only note silently the conversation between the two. If successful, new insights will emerge.

Guided philosophical imagery

The technique of guided imagery is sometimes used in various kinds of psychotherapy and spiritual groups. Here it is adapted to contemplative philosophy. The basic idea is that our spontaneous imagery can give voice to deep understandings that are not easily accessible to our conscious verbal thinking.

Choose a short philosophical text in which the central idea can be metaphorically visualized. An example is Plato's cave allegory, in which we can visualize the cave-dwellers and their way out to the sun; or Nietzsche's passage "Three metamorphoses" in which self-transformation is likened to a camel who changes to a lion, and the lion to a child.[5]

Sit straight but comfortably on a chair or on the floor in a symmetric position. Read the text slowly to understand its surface meaning. After you have understood the text, read it a few more times while

---

5. Plato, *Republic*, Book 7; Friedrich Nietzsche, *Thus Spoke Zarathustra* in Walter Kaufmann, *The Portable Nietzsche*, Penguin Books, 1984, Part I, 137-140.

attending to the visual images suggested by the text. This repeated reading can serve as a centering exercise.

Now that the text is clear and your mind is quiet and focused, close your eyes. In your imagination visualize yourself inside the imaginary landscape suggested by the text. For example, in the case of Plato's cave allegory, you might imagine yourself sitting on a chair inside the cave and watching the shadows on the wall. You may imagine the texture and color of the walls, the chair, the movement of the shadows, and your fellow prisoners sitting next to you.

Once you have imagined where you are, set your imagination free and let it explore by itself what will happen. In the case of Plato's cave, for example, you can imagine yourself standing up, turning around and walking towards the exit – and at this point let your imagination decide what will happen outside the cave.

Do not dictate to your imagination what it should imagine – let it move along spontaneously, taking you wherever it wishes. Your natural tendency to try to control your mind should be pushed aside, so that your only role would be to silently witness the imaginary journey and remember it. After ten or fifteen minutes, when you feel that you are ready to end the journey, find an appropriate place to stop (on a hill outside the cave, for example), and gently bring yourself back to yourself. Open your eyes gently when the time feels right.

Now, with your eyes open, reflect on your imaginary journey. What has it revealed to you? What shape did it give to the ideas in the text, and to your own ideas? Did the things you saw and felt symbolize insightful ideas? Was there anything surprising, new, enlightening in those ideas? You may want to write down the answers to these questions in a free, spontaneous way.

Calligraphic contemplation

This is an open and unstructured procedure. Read the text slowly and silently, and note a sentence (or a short passage) that attracts your attention and that "wants to tell you something" as it were. Write this sentence on a sheet of special paper in precise, beautiful letters, using a calligraphic pen. Focus your mind on the writing of the letters and treat them as precious. The focused writing can induce in you a sense of inner silence, attentiveness, and preciousness. This may yield new insights about the ideas in the text.

To do this exercise, you don't need to be a professional calligrapher. A beginner can do it just as well. The goal is not to produce professional scripts, but to enter an inner state of contemplative attentiveness.

Chapter 7

TYPICAL CONTEMPLATIVE EXPERIENCES

Any of the above procedures may create deep insights. These insights are "deep" in the sense that they open us to hidden aspects of our reality, but also in the sense that they awaken within us an inner dimension, or depth, from which we can appreciate these aspects. Both of these impacts usually involve meaningful experiences.

Contemplators report a wide range of contemplative experiences, and it is impossible to describe or classify them with precision. Nevertheless, let me list in this chapter some of the more common experiences. If you have had similar experiences, you will find them easier to understand.

Most of these deep experiences are enjoyable. It is tempting to fall in love with them and try replicating them again and again. But it is important to remember that our purpose in contemplation is to connect to the depth of our reality, not just to enjoy good feelings. Sweet experiences can do good things – they can give us energy and motivation, but they are not the main goal of contemplation.

Inner stillness

Perhaps the most common experience in contemplation is a strong sense of inner silence or stillness, which replaces the usual noisy activity of our mind. In fact, we are so used to this ongoing inner noise that we realize its existence only after experiencing its absence. This does not mean that we stop thinking and behaving. We may experience inner silence even in the middle of a conversation. Inner silence is not an absence but an intense presence. We sense it filling our mind like a transparent substance. Often it feels like a space that envelops us, so that everything we do is suspended in this silent space: Our thoughts, the rhythm of our actions, our bodily posture.

The experience of inner silence strengthens the impact of our thoughts and insights. They no longer feel as insignificant private chatter, but as part of a greater realm in which we participate.

Preciousness and sacredness

Another common experience is that of preciousness. We experience the insights that arise in our mind as having a great value, as precious, even as sacred – not because they are useful for something else, not because they are enjoyable, but because they possess the quality of preciousness. The experience is similar to what we feel when we enter the sacred space of a temple, or when we stand at the top of a mountain and look with awe at the immensity of the landscape. It is not simply an experience of "I am enjoying it" but of being in a special space that is elevated above ordinary matters.

The bubble experience

An important contemplative experience is what can be called a "bubble" of insight. This happens when an insight appears in our awareness unexpected, feeling as if it came from elsewhere, as if it rose from some hidden depth, just as a bubble of air rises from the dark bottom of a lake towards the visible surface of the water.

The insight itself may be somewhat vague at first, and it may take some effort to verbalize it in words. When we manage to translate it into words, the words may feel inadequate, unable to capture the original insight, sometimes even banal and trivial. Yet, the original insight, before having been translated into words, had felt meaningful and precious as if it came from a deeper source wisdom.

Bubbles of insight need not be powerful and earth-shaking. On the contrary, they are often barely noticeable, fluttering on the periphery of our awareness. Yet, when we notice them we realize that they feel different from ordinary thoughts, and that they have a special kind of realness and significance.

The bubble experience is important for contemplation because it is more than a mere feeling – it also involves an understanding of a fundamental issue. Bubbles sometimes appear in everyday situations as well, outside the specific context of contemplation, but we usually fail to notice them because they are faint and fleeting. Contemplation has the double function of helping them appear, and also helping us notice them.

The inner depth experience

Somewhat more intense than the bubble experience is the experience of inner depth. Here, not only do we experience an understanding coming into us from "elsewhere," we also experience this "elsewhere" within us, usually as a dormant, hidden aspect of our being that is being awakened or revealed. We then feel as if the familiar self – so familiar that we hardly ever bother to think about it – is just a superficial crust over a deeper self. In this newly discovered depth, we find a source of inspiration that generates understandings that are especially powerful and clear.

This sense of a new depth is temporary, and it disappears not long after the contemplation. But it leaves us with a vivid realization that we are deeper than we normally seem to be.

The Lu experience

As mentioned earlier, we sometimes feel as if touched by something bigger than ourselves, something more real or even ultimate. We feel as if a greater or higher reality is touching us, enveloping us, filling and invading us, sometimes infusing into us inspiring energies and thoughts. Often this greater reality induces in us a sense of awe, wonder, and preciousness.

It is tempting to interpret this experience as an encounter with a higher being or even God. Indeed, such an experience has been reported by many mystics in many religious traditions and interpreted as communication with a divine being. For us, however, it is better to avoid metaphysical speculations. It is enough to remain faithful to the experience itself and talk about a sense of a higher reality. As I have already said, I myself call it the Lu experience, where "Lu" is a word without meaning, as appropriate to a reality that leaves us speechless.

Variety of experiences

The above list includes some of the more typical experiences that may accompany contemplation, but of course it is not exhaustive. There are additional kinds of contemplative experiences. What is especially important about them is that they involve a profound (though temporary) change in our state of mind and give us a heightened sense of realness, understanding, and connectedness to a fundamental dimension of reality.

Chapter 8

AFTER CONTEMPLATING

When we approach the end of the contemplation session, it is important not to end it too abruptly. Ending it gently allows the mind to digest and integrate the contemplative experience, reflect on its meaning, and take from it whatever has been valuable. This can be done in one of several short procedures at the end of the session.

Calligraphic reflection

If you have some ability to write calligraphy, even if you are a mere beginner, then a good ending of the session is sitting down quietly and writing a selected sentence or sentences from the text. While writing, try not to think – simply write the words letter by letter carefully and slowly. The important thing here is not the product but the writing process. This is why your calligraphic skills are not important. Your mind, being focused on the writing action, will maintain the contemplative silence, which will help digesting the impact of the session.

Insights sketch

To summarize the insights you have gained during the session, sit down quietly with a sheet of paper and reflect on the session. When you recall a meaningful idea from the session, draw it in a simple, schematic sketch. Don't plan too much and don't calculate – let your hand do the drawing. Try to avoid excessive details, but you may add a couple of explanatory words next to some of the elements in the sketch (for instance, the word "flow of time" next to a sketch of a river). The sketch is intended to serve as a simple reminder of the idea, not a detailed representation of it.

For example, if you recall a distinction which you had made during the session between the lightness of beauty and heaviness of goodness, you may draw them as a circle and a pyramid. You may add the word "beauty" inside the circle, and the word "goodness" inside the pyramid.

Draw each idea on a small part of the page, and then draw the next idea in a different area. In this way you will produce an array of several sketches that are distributed over the sheet of paper. It is best to draw spontaneously without too much planning, and without trying to unify the different sketches into one single drawing covering the entire page.

The process of drawing will allow you to quietly bring to your mind the different insights you have gained during the session, and to integrate them together without forcing them into an artificial conclusion.

Presencing walk

After contemplating you may take a walk, preferably in nature. Maintain the contemplative spirit and gently bring to your mind the insights and experiences from the session, letting them float in your consciousness without imposing on them analyses or interpretations.

In order to maintain the spirit of quiet contemplation, you can turn your walk into a presencing walk – a walk in which you are fully aware of your body, your thoughts, and your environment. (As mentioned before, "presencing" means making something present in your awareness.) The following three guidelines may help to make this walk effective:

First, gentleness: Whatever you do with your body or mind, do it gently. Avoid abruptness. Walk gently, turn your eyes gently, move your arms gently. You may touch gently a stone, a leaf, the ground.

Second, peripheral vision: Instead of focusing your eyes on a specific object, try spreading your visual attention over your entire field of vision.

Third, presencing: Whatever you see, hear, or feel, make it present in your consciousness.

Don't force these three guidelines, but rather flow with them. They should not be a distraction but helpers in making you attentive and quiet.

Keeping a reminder within

The above endings may take ten or twenty minutes, more or less, immediately after the contemplation session. You may also do a longer exercise that stretches over several hours. To do so, choose a sentence that touched you meaningfully during the contemplation, or formulate a new one. Now, for the rest of the day, try keeping the sentence in your mind. You do not have to think about it explicitly, just keep it in the background of your thoughts.

Naturally, you will quickly be distracted by everyday matters, probably for long stretches of time. This is completely acceptable. But whenever you notice that you have lost it, recollect yourself and recite the sentence a couple of times in your mind. You may also make a simple gesture – touching your heart, bowing your head, etc. – as a sign of recollection and acknowledgement.

While doing all this, a new "bubble" of insight might appear in your mind, perhaps resonating with the selected sentence or responding it. Notice it gently as if you have received a gift.

Chapter 9

THE PHILOSOPHICAL CONTEMPLATOR

Philosophical contemplation is not equally accessible to everybody. In order to become a philosophical contemplator, it helps to have certain sensitivities and inclinations, and to some extent a certain background and experience. For some people these qualities come naturally, others need to awaken them, while still others must develop them with an effort.

Openness to ideas

An important quality is openness to ideas – not necessarily a desire to accumulate philosophical knowledge, but a flexible mind that can experiment with new ideas without getting stuck in opinions and biases. This means that you are able to overcome the human need to judge and declare and agree or disagree, and that you can reflect with genuine willingness to go wherever your reflections will take you. The opposite of openness is being rigid and stubborn in your thoughts, or in short opinionated. If you are opinionated, you cling to certain opinions and refuse to seriously and honestly consider any alternative. If you are truly open to ideas, you can wander in the landscape of ideas without preconditions, without agreeing or disagreeing, without knowing in advance where you must end up.

This should not be as difficult as it might seem. Contemplation does not require you to change your personal views and agree with the text, but rather to put on hold your views and truly listen to new ideas.

Passion for philosophical inquiry

Philosophical ideas have a tremendous power to inspire us, to move us, enlighten us. The problem is that many people treat philosophical ideas as an abstract matter, and they have little interest in them. But for the philosophical contemplator, philosophical ideas are a precious source of life.

To be a philosophical contemplator you must find meaning and significance in the philosophical inquiry. This does not simply mean that you "enjoy" reading philosophy, or that you "like" talking about it. Passion is much more than mere enjoyment or interest. It means that the big issues of life are important and meaningful to you, and that they can move you and inspire you.

What is the meaning of life? What is true love? What is truth? While some people might dismiss such issues as idle questions or as mere entertainment, others find them moving and important. For them, life without exploring these issues is shallow and incomplete.

If you are philosophically minded, then philosophical ideas are alive in you. This does not require you to have a strong belief in a particular theory – a living philosophical idea is not a dogma to cling to. On the contrary, a philosophical conviction that is settled like a finished product is not alive. It is alive in you if it keeps baffling and intriguing you, generating in your mind new insights and considerations, and acquiring new meanings and implications. A living philosophical idea is a seed of new evolving understandings that occupy your thoughts, at least from time to time.

The philosophical contemplator is, therefore, somebody who treats philosophical ideas as a serious matter, and who lets them resonate within him throughout his life. He does not necessarily have a theory about life, or an opinion about this or that philosophical issue, but he is attuned to philosophical ideas as a living fountain within him. His everyday life includes an ongoing dialogue with them.

Yearning

To be a philosophical contemplator you must also have a yearning to understand life and reality. You must be a seeker – somebody who searches for meaning, for truth, for a sense of realness and depth.

Yearning is not the same as desiring. When we desire something – a cake, or money, or sex – we want to use the object for our own satisfaction; we want to get hold of the object and bring it to us. In contrast, in yearning the movement is in the opposite direction: We want to go out of ourselves toward what we yearn for, we want to give ourselves to it.

Yearning in this sense is probably quite rare. Many people want to be happy, to attain money or power or fame, to develop themselves, but all these are not the same as yearning. In fact, they are almost its opposite. In yearning the central issue is not satisfying your needs but reaching out outside yourself towards whatever it is that you yearn for. To yearn is like being in love: Your heart goes out to the beloved. Just as the true lover is ready to sacrifice happiness for the sake of the beloved, a person who yearns is not concerned about himself but about what he yearns for.

To be a true contemplator you must be somebody who yearns. Your yearning does not have to torture you incessantly, but it must be in the background of your life. If you practice contemplation exercises merely because you want to entertain yourself, or to feel good, or improve your abilities, then you are not fully contemplating. Contemplating is an act of stepping out of yourself, out of your needs, out of your self-centered world.

Thus, a philosophical contemplator is a seeker. You are a seeker if you are at home when you inquire, when you are on the way, not when you find an answer. This means that you are looking for something different from what satisfies most people: a good salary, a stable marriage, possessions, reputation, power, comfort. A seeker is always in search. Searching is his way of being, not a temporary stage until he finds what he wants. He yearns for a higher kind of life, he yearns to be in touch with truth and reality, and such yearnings are never satisfied. True seeking is a way of being.

The contemplative disposition

Many people are truly interested in philosophy, but they have no inclination for contemplation. They may be very good at discussing basic questions, they may be fascinated by theories about the world, but they always maintain an attitude of an academic thinker, an analyzer, an observer who looks at ideas intellectually.

There is nothing wrong with this attitude, but it is not the attitude of a contemplator. A contemplator has the ability and inclination to resonate *with* ideas, not just to think *about* them.

This is not a usual way of relating to ideas. It does not require mere smartness or logical thinking, but rather attentiveness to one's inwardness and sensitivity to one's inner depth, somewhat like the poet. This is why a good academic philosopher is not necessarily a good contemplator, and vice versa. The two are engaged in different states of mind that involve different abilities and sensitivities. Nevertheless, the two are not opposed. The combination of good analytic capacities and contemplative tendencies can be powerful indeed.

Chapter 10

TEXTS FOR CONTEMPLATION

The following are two examples of philosophical texts that are appropriate for contemplation. They are condensed and not too long, and they relate to aspects of everyday life. Note that they have both been slightly modified in order to make them more readable.

More texts can be found on the "Philosophical Topics" page of my Agora website at: https://philopractice.org

From "Meditations" by Marcus Aurelius[6]

Marcus Aurelius (121-180 AD) was a Philosopher and a Roman emperor from the Stoic school of philosophy. As a Stoic, he emphasized the importance of maintaining inner peace, accepting fate calmly, freedom from the power of emotions, and being in harmony with the cosmos.

The following passages are from Marcus Aurelius' book *Meditations*, which was in fact a personal notebook where he wrote his personal reflections. Those passages tell us that the true self - "the guiding principle" or "the daemon" (sometimes translated as

---

6. Adapted from Marcus Aurelius, *Meditations*, translated by George Long, Blackie & Son, London 1910.

"the ruling faculty") – is the rational faculty within the person. It is the element within us which follows Reason, which sees the larger perspective on things, thinks calmly, is undisturbed by emotions and free from emotional attachment. When we follow this inner guide, we are true to our human nature, and are in harmony with the Logos that rules the Cosmos.

From BOOK 2

9. You must always bear in mind what is the nature of the whole cosmos, and what is my own nature, and how the first is related to the second, and what kind of a part I am in the whole. And there is nobody who stops you from always doing and saying the things that are according to the nature of the whole, of which you are a part.

17. Everything which belongs to the body is a stream, and what belongs to the soul is a dream and vapor, and life is a war and a foreigner's sojourn, and after fame comes oblivion. What, then, can guide a person? One and only one thing – philosophy. But this consists in keeping the daemon that is within you free from violence and unharmed, superior to pains and pleasures, doing nothing without purpose, without falsity or hypocrisy, without relying on anybody else to do or not to do anything. And also, accepting all that happens, and all that is assigned to you, as coming from wherever you yourself came. And, finally, waiting for death with a cheerful mind, accepting it as no more than a dissolution of the elements of which every living being is made.

From BOOK 7

16. The guiding principle does not disturb itself; it does not frighten itself or causes itself pain. [...] The guiding principle in itself desires nothing, unless it creates a desire for itself. Therefore, it is free from disturbance and is not stopped by anything, unless it disturbs or stops itself.

28. Retire into yourself. The rational principle which rules is by nature content with itself when it does what is just, and in doing so it achieves tranquility.

From BOOK 8

43. Different things delight different people. But it is my delight to keep the guiding principle sound without turning away either from any person or from any things that happen to people, but looking at, and accepting everything with welcome eyes, and using everything according to its value.

48. Remember that the guiding principle is invincible. When it is self-collected, it is satisfied with itself, if it does nothing which it does not choose to do [...] Therefore, the mind which is free from passions is a citadel, because a person has nothing more secure to which he can escape. Anybody who has not seen this is ignorant, but anybody who has seen it and does not escape to this refuge is unhappy.

2. From "The Over-Soul" by Emerson[7]

Ralph Waldo Emerson (1803-1882) was an American philosopher, writer and poet, who was the leader of the Transcendentalist movement of the 19th century. The following are selected passages from his essay "The Over-Soul" (some sentences slightly simplified). For Emerson, the "over-soul" is a higher dimension of existence which is the source of inspiration, goodness, beauty, and wisdom.

Man is a stream whose source is hidden. Our being descends into us from we know not where. The most exact calculator cannot predict that something incalculable may not happen the very next moment. I am forced every moment to acknowledge a higher origin of events than the will which I call "mine."

As with events, so is it with thoughts. When I watch that flowing river which, out of regions I don't see, pours for a while its streams into me, I see that I am a pensioner – not a cause, but a surprised spectator of this ethereal water; that I may desire and search and be receptive, but from some alien energy the visions come. [...]

We live in succession, in division, in parts, in particles. Meantime, within each person is the soul of the whole, the wise silence, the universal beauty, to which every part and

---

7. Adapted from Ralph Waldo Emerson, *Essays and English Traits*, "The Over-soul," Collier, New York 1909, 137-139.

particle is equally related, the eternal one. *And this deep power in which we exist, and whose beatitude is all accessible to us, is not only self-sufficient and perfect in every hour; furthermore, the act of seeing and the thing that is seen, the seer and the spectacle, the subject and the object, are one. […]*

All goes to show that the soul in a person is not an organ, but animates and exercises all the organs. It is not a function – like the power of memory, of calculation, of comparison, but it uses these as hands and feet. It is not a faculty, but a light. It is not the intellect or the will, but the master of the intellect and the will, the background of our being in which they lie — an immensity that is not possessed and that cannot be possessed. From within or from behind, a light shines through us upon things and makes us aware that we are nothing but the light is all. A person is the façade of a temple where all wisdom and all good dwell.

www.ingramcontent.com/pod-product-compliance
Lightning Source LLC
Chambersburg PA
CBHW071536080526
44588CB00011B/1694